LETTERS HOME
from
CHINA

Marcia S. Gresko

BLACKBIRCH PRESS, INC.
WOODBRIDGE, CONNECTICUT

Published by Blackbirch Press, Inc.
260 Amity Road
Woodbridge, CT 06525

©1999 by Blackbirch Press, Inc.
First Edition

e-mail: staff@blackbirch.com
Web site: www.blackbirch.com

Printed in Singapore

10 9 8 7 6 5 4 3 2 1

All photographs ©Corel Corporation

                    Library of Congress Cataloging-in-Publication Data
Gresko, Marcia S.
China / Marcia S. Gresko.
    p.   cm. — (Letters home from . . .)
Includes bibliographical references and index.
Summary: Describes some of the sights and experiences on a trip through China, including visits to Beijing, the Great Wall, Taiyuan, Shanghai, and Hangzhou.
ISBN 1-56711-400-8
1. Gresko, Marcia S.—Journeys—China—Juvenile literature. 2. China—Description and travel—Juvenile literature. [1. China—Description and travel.] I. Title. II. Series.
DS712.G74   1999   98-52405
915.104'59—dc21   CIP
                                                                        AC

TABLE OF CONTENTS

Arrival in . . .

Beijing

After more than 13 hours in the air, we finally arrived in Beijing. This city, in northeastern China, has been the country's capital on and off for more than 2,000 years! It has had many different names, depending on who ruled it.

We're spending several weeks in China because it's so huge. It's the third-largest country in the world! Only Russia and Canada are bigger.

One out of every five people in the world lives in China! More than 1.2 billion people live here. That's more than in any other country in the world.

As our taxi made its way toward the hotel, it was easy to see why China is called the Kingdom of Bicycles. Our driver told us people ride bicycles everywhere. There are more bicycles in China than there are people in the United States!

Beijing

Yesterday we started out in the center of Beijing, at Tiananmen Square. It's the world's biggest public square. Beijing is home to more than 9 million people.

We spent the whole day in the Forbidden City. This was home to the emperors who ruled China long ago. It was surrounded by a moat and high, red walls. Its gates were guarded by huge lion statues. Ordinary people were not allowed inside. Now it is open to everyone. Many of its palaces have been turned into museums. We saw the golden Dragon Throne. That's where the Emperor sat. He was thought to be the Son of Heaven.

Courtyard, Forbidden City

Billboard, Beijing

的社会义物质文明和精神文明而奋斗

Horsedrawn carts, countryside near Beijing

Lion, Forbidden City

Our guide said that Beijing is really two cities in one. Outside the Forbidden City are narrow alleys lined with one-story cement houses. Peddlers sell tea and snacks. Market stalls sell everything from fresh fruits and vegetables to pottery and books. Modern Beijing has wide streets lined with skyscrapers, department stores, hospitals, theaters, and restaurants. There are factories, tall government buildings, and new apartment houses.

Tomorrow, we're going to visit one of the most beautiful parks in Beijing at the Summer Palace.

Beijing

Today we went boating on beautiful Lake Kunming. The lake is part of the Summer Palace where the royal family went to escape Beijing's hot weather.

Our guide explained that ancient China was not one country, but a number of rival kingdoms. About 2,000 years ago, these kingdoms were united by China's first emperor, Prince Sheng. Prince Sheng was a member of the Qin dynasty, or ruling family. The name China came from Qin. Chinese history is divided into periods named after the ruling dynasty.

Bridge at the Summer Palace

Carved fence

Decorated roof, Summer Palace

Dynasties could last a few years or several hundred years. Under them, Chinese civilization made great progress. The Chinese invented paper, the compass, the wheelbarrow, movable type for printing, fine pottery called porcelain, and gunpowder. No wonder during holidays they use so many fireworks!

The royal family lived in splendor. The peaceful resort is filled with gardens, towers, halls, and bridges. The Long Corridor is a grand covered walkway. Its ceilings show paintings of birds, flowers, famous landscapes, and scenes from Chinese history and fairy tales.

Our sightseeing made us very hungry, so we stuffed ourselves on delicious dumplings in a restaurant that was once a royal theater.

The Great Wall

We took the bus north from Beijing today to see one of the wonders of the world—the Great Wall of China. It's huge! It twists and turns like a snake over more than 4,000 miles of mountains and deserts in northern China. The guidebook says it's the longest structure ever built on earth. It is so long that it can be seen from the moon!

Top of Great Wall, Badalin

Great Wall, Pa-ta-ling Area, Shanxi

Great Wall

Our tour guide said that the Great Wall is more than 2,000 years old. She explained that it was begun by China's first emperor to protect his empire from invasion. Almost one million people worked for 10 years to build the mighty wall. Peasants were marched off their farms to work on it. And prisoners were forced to do the most difficult and dangerous construction. Chinese legend says that workers who were caught trying to run away were buried alive inside the wall (yikes!).

Nearly one million soldiers once guarded the wall. They lived in large forts built along the wall. We made the long, cold climb up to one of the forts. I know it was just the wind, but when I closed my eyes, I thought I heard arrows whistling and swords clanging.

Taiyuan

After the Great Wall, we traveled south about 250 miles to our next stop—Taiyuan. This is the capital of the Shanxi province. Shanxi means "west of the mountains." Most of the province is a mountainous region.

On the way, our tour guide told us about Taiyuan's long, bloody history. The city is located on a route taken by northern invaders who entered China. There were so many battles fought in ancient Taiyuan that the city once had 27 temples dedicated to the god of war!

A beautiful lake, Taiyuan

Carved lintel, Chin Temple

Stairway, Chin Temple

Our destination—the Chin Temple—is just outside the city. The temple was built by Prince Shu Yu in honor of his mother. Worshipping dead ancestors from long ago was an important part of Chinese culture. It is still practiced in parts of China today.

The oldest and most beautiful of the temple buildings is the Sacred Mother Hall. Ferocious wooden dragons snarl from large pillars at the entrance. The dragon is an important symbol of power and wealth in Chinese culture.

Taiyuan's scenery is a mixture of old and new. Factories produce iron and steel, cement, chemicals, and heavy machinery like tractors. In the countryside, farms produce crops of grains and fruits.

Daily Life

It seems there's always something happening in the streets of a Chinese city! When we left for the museum this morning, the parks were filled with people exercising. The streets were crowded with vendors and commuters on their way to work. In most Chinese families, both parents work six days a week. Children go to school six days a week, too! After school, some students go to the Children's Palace. That's a place to study art or dance, learn an instrument, or compete in sports. In China's cities, it is common for grandparents to live in the same small apartment as their children and grandchildren. China has such a large population, families are encouraged to have just one child each.

Excercising with T'ai Chi

Chinese money

Street vendors in Sian

Poster (one family, one child)

Children in Village Square

Morning excercises in Shanghai

At the museum we admired some of China's traditional arts and crafts. There were colorful porcelain bowls, fancy carved boxes, and ancient jade figures. I liked the scenes of mountains, water, trees, and birds painted on long scrolls. Our guide read aloud a poem that came with one of the paintings. It was written in a fine Chinese brush-writing called calligraphy. The Chinese writing system uses characters instead of letters. Each character stands for a whole word or syllable. Here is how you write "happy birthday": 生日快乐.

Shanghai

Today we visited one of the largest cities in the world—Shanghai. More than 12 million people live here. That's roughly the number of people that live in the state of Pennsylvania!

Shanghai is located about 700 miles from Taiyuan. It's on the Huang Po River on the southeastern coast of China. The mighty Yangtze River is close by. That's the world's third-longest river. Shanghai's location near these important waterways makes it China's leading port.

Barge boat loaded with hay, near Shanghai

Barges on a canal, near Shanghai

Brocade factory, Shanghai

Loom, Shanghai

Shanghai is China's industrial capital. It is also one of the world's leading manufacturing centers. Factories produce iron, steel, heavy machinery, and electronic equipment. We visited a textile factory where we saw beautiful cloth, called brocade, being made.

Outside the city is the country's best farm land. Farming is very important in China. When you visit a crowded city like Shanghai, it's hard to believe that most Chinese people live and work on farms. Farmers around Shanghai grow grains, fruits, and vegetables. Barges take these products to the city on canals.

Tonight we're going to see the world-famous Shanghai Acrobatic Troupe!

Hangzhou

We arrived by train in Hangzhou yesterday. The famous explorer, Marco Polo, called it the "noblest and most beautiful city on earth."

Hangzhou is located about 100 miles southwest of Shanghai. It's in the fertile Yangtze River delta. We passed terraced hillsides planted with rows and rows of tea bushes. Tea grows well in the warm, humid climate here. China is one of the world's leading tea producers. They also drink a whole lot of it!

West Lake

Tea cultivation

Water lillies

West Lake

In Hangzhou we headed for West Lake. That's China's most famous lake. The guidebook said that West Lake was created when a dike was built to protect the city from flooding. But, I like our guide's tale of how it was formed better. She said that a selfish sky goddess stole a beautiful pearl from two magical creatures—a phoenix and a dragon. When they tried to rescue it, the glowing pearl fell to earth and became West Lake. The loyal phoenix and dragon became the two mountains beside the lake, guarding their pearl forever.

Guilin

Today we took a plane southwest from Hangzhou to Guilin in mountainous southeastern China. The trip was about 700 miles. The scenery looked just like the beautiful painted scrolls we'd seen in shops and museums.

We had to hurry to catch the boat for our trip down the Li River. Rivers are an important way to travel in China. Boats carry large numbers of passengers and farm crops from one part of the country to another.

The trip took about five hours. There was so much to see that it seemed shorter. The most exciting sight was the fishermen using trained birds, called cormorants, to make their catch. The birds dive into the water, trap fish in

Guilin

Li River

Water buffalo eating weeds, Li River

Fisherman, Li River

Rice field

their beaks, and bring them back to the boats! With more than 50,000 rivers and 3,500 miles of coastline, China has one of the world's largest fishing industries.

Then we saw a water buffalo enjoying its lunch and a swim in the river. Water buffalo are still used to plow the fields that grow the area's main crop—rice. Our guide said we'd probably see many more of China's animals at our next stop—Yunan.

Yunan

Our flight west from Guilin to Yunan only took about an hour. Yunan is the fourth largest of China's 22 provinces, or states. We're staying in its capital city—Kunming.

Our guide told us that during our visit to Yunan we'll see more kinds of scenery, animals, plants, and people than we have seen during the whole rest of our trip!

There are icy mountains in the northwest and rainforest jungles in the south. That's where Yunan borders the countries of Laos and Vietnam. Yunan farmers grow many kinds of crops, from rice and tea to tobacco and sugar cane.

Gateway, street market, Kunming

Gateway to city, Dali

Buddhist temple, Dal Lake

Old woman at market, Dali Area

Half of all the kinds of animals and plants that live in China can be found in Yunan. There are elephants and tigers, rhinos and peacocks, bears and snow leopards! Valuable plants that are important to Chinese medicine grow in the mountains.

There are also 24 different ethnic groups in Yunan. Many have their own language, religion, dress, and way of life.

Kunming is known as the "Spring City" because of its year-round good weather. Like many Chinese cities, Kunming is a mixture of old and new. There are mills and factories, as well as temples and tea houses.

Yunan

We got an early start Tuesday for our long bus ride to the Dali region west of Kunming. We're going there for the Third Moon Street Fair. People from all over the province come to buy, sell, sing, dance, and race horses.

Our bus zigzagged through hills and mountains before we reached scenic Erhai (Ear) Lake, where Dali is located. Dali is the home of the Bai people.

Woman practicing T'ai Chi

Woman in traditional dress

Young girls in Lijiang

Rape-seed fields

Traditional Chinese pagoda

Many Bai make their living by fishing, but most are hard-working rice farmers. Beans, wheat, and rape-seed (used to make oil) also grow in the fertile soil. Farm work is still done by hand, as it has been for centuries.

The stalls at the fair were piled high with everything from noodles and meat to fancy embroidered hats, shirts, and shoes. We joined the crowds who'd come from all over China to buy the rare herbs grown in Yunan's far away mountains. Our guide explained that many Chinese people still use traditional herbal medicines. Many Chinese use herbs to cure almost everything—from stomach aches to sleeplessness to bruises!

Tibet

Tashi delag (hello) from Tibet! I'm in far southwestern China!
   Our tour guide told us that people call Tibet the "Roof of the World" because it's in the highest part of the whole planet!
   Most of Tibet is a high, empty plateau covered by rocky desert and lonely plains. Snow-covered mountains surround us on three sides. Five of the world's tallest mountains are located in the Himalayas, on the border of Tibet and Nepal. Mt. Everest is the most famous. It's the world's highest peak (more than 5 1/2 miles high!). The Tibetan name for it means "Goddess Mother of the World."

Town buildings, Shigatse, Tibet

Young Tibetan women

Young Tibetan boy

Himalayan Mountains

Mountains in Eastern Tibet

Tibet has more than 1,000 lakes. Many are so salty, no fish can live in them. Legend says that they are the tears of a goddess. Tibet also has small areas of forest and grasslands where deer, tigers, bears, monkeys, and wild horses live.

Most Tibetans are either farmers or nomads. Nomads wander the wilderness looking for good lands on which to graze their herds of yaks, sheep, and goats. They carry all their belongings on the strong backs of their shaggy yaks! Our guide explained that nomadic tribes live mostly in the northern and eastern plains.

Lhasa

On Thursday we explored Lhasa, the capital of Tibet.
Everywhere you go you can see the gleaming golden rooftops of the
Potala Palace. Our guide told us it was the winter home of the Dalai Lama,
the religious leader of the Tibetan people. When Tibet was taken over by
China, the Dalai Lama fled to India to avoid being captured.
The palace is like a gigantic maze. It is 13 stories high. It's also the tallest
palace in the world! There are more than 1,000 rooms connected by

Old Central City, Lhasa

Potala, Lhasa

Prayer wheels at
Dreprung monastery

Beautiful Tibetan
landscape

dark, twisting hallways. There are 10,000 altars and 200,000 statues! The jewel-covered tombs of eight Dalai Lamas are here, too.

Outside the palace, we rented bicycles and peddled to the Old Central City. In the marketplace, stalls were crammed with hand-woven rugs, jewelry, yak meat, and magic charms. We bargained for a hand-held prayer wheel—a small version of the huge ones we'd seen on buildings. Inside the cylinders are pieces of paper with prayers on them. Every turn of the wheel equals saying a prayer.

Our guide told us that Tibetans have been called the most religious people in the world. They practice Buddhism, a 2,000-year-old religion from India.

Buddhism

Today our guide was a young Buddhist monk. He explained that Buddhism was founded by a prince who spent his life as a wandering monk, searching for inner peace and happiness. After traveling for six years, the prince found the way to reach nirvana—a state of heavenly peace. People soon began calling him Buddha. That means Enlightened One.

Buddhists believe that peace and happiness come from living a simple life and helping others.

Buddhists also believe that each time a person dies, the soul is reborn in a new body. A person who lives a good life may be reborn as a teacher or wise leader. A person who lives badly may be reborn as an animal, or even as an insect! The soul is reborn many times on its way to nirvana.

Courtyard of Buddhist Monastery

Young Dai
Buddhist Monk

Young monk,
Lhasa

From inside the monastery we could smell the spicy smoke of burning juniper branches. In the flickering, yellow light of yak-butter candles, we looked up at the towering statues of gods and demons. Buddhists believe in many god-like spirits. The god of mercy is one of the most important. Our guide gave us a white silk scarf, called a kata, to drape around one of the statues as a gift.

We told him "thuk ji chay" (thank you) for a wonderful day.

Glossary

Ancestors family members that lived a long time ago, usually several generations back.

Brocade fabric woven in a raised pattern.

Civilization an advanced stage of human organization, technology, or culture.

Dike a large wall or dam that is built to hold back water and prevent flooding.

Dynasty a series of rulers belonging to the same family.

Empire a group of countries that all have the same ruler.

Fertile condition of land that is good for growing crops.

Moat a deep, wide ditch dug all around a building or city and filled with water to prevent attack.

Peddler someone who travels around selling things.

Square an open area in a town or city, often used as a park, that is surrounded by streets on all four sides.

For More Information

Books

Cheong, Colin. Elizabeth Berg (Editor). *China* (Festivals of the World). Milwaukee, WI: Gareth Stevens, 1997.

Enderlein, Cheryl L. *Celebrating Birthdays in China* (Birthdays Around the World). Danbury, CT: Grolier Publications, 1998.

Patkanen, Matti A. *The Children of China* (The World's Children). Minneapolis, MN: Carolrhoda Books, 1990.

Web Sites

Tour of China

Visit many of the main cities of China—
www.ihep.ac.cn/tour/china_tour.html.

National Palace Museum

Learn about Chinese culture and history—
www.npm.gov.tw/index.htm.

Index